by

James Walton

THE DALESMAN PUBLISHING COMPANY LTD., CLAPHAM (Via Lancaster), NORTH YORKSHIRE.

First Published 1947

New Impression 1979

© James Walton, 1947, 1979

ISBN : 0 85206 505 1

Printed in Great Britain by
GEO TODD & SON,
Marlborough Street, Whitehaven.

Contents

Foreword
By John Miller

THE traditional homesteads erected before the Industrial Revolution are some of the country's most attractive buildings. Until recent years, historians have paid little attention to them preferring instead the larger country houses and mansions. This is surprising for they survive in far larger numbers and are the dominating feature in the landscape. Most of them were built during the 17th and 18th centuries, and in many cases replaced earlier homesteads. Their charm is due, in part, to the use of local materials which belong organically to the landscape, and to the inherited skills of generations of craftsmen. They remain now as fascinating records of a way of life that has long since disappeared.

James Walton, the author of *Homesteads in the Yorkshire Dales,* is widely known as one of the early pioneers in the study of traditional buildings — a movement whose origins can be traced back to the late 1890s with the work of two notable scholars, S. O. Addy and C. F. Innocent. His prolific writings follow on from these early researchers and began in the 1930s when he was living in the West Riding of Yorkshire, which by coincidence was the area where S. O. Addy and C. F. Innocent had made their recordings. By the early 1950s interest in the subject was growing simultaneously and independently in other parts of the country, and Mr. Walton became a founder member of a society (later to be known as the Vernacular Architecture Group) formed to put researchers in touch with each other. It was also about this time that he went to live in South Africa, where he still resides, and where he has founded the South African Vernacular Group. (1).

Homesteads of the Yorkshire Dales, published in 1947, has deservedly been described as a model regional study and has been widely used by recent investigators. Despite some more recent publications, notably by A. Raistrick and Marie Hartley and Joan Ingilby, it still remains an authoritative introduction to Dales building, and its reprinting will be welcomed by serious students of vernacular architecture. The opening chapter gives a very clear account of the first settlers in the Dales and the mark they made on the landscape. Subsequent chapters show how their ideas and primitive forms of construction were adapted and incorporated by later occupiers during the major rebuilding programme in the 17th and 18th centuries. The author

(1) Vernacular Architecture Group, Vol. 5, 1974.

avoids the trap of concentrating only on the more spectacular 17th century reconstructions, and devotes a whole chapter to the evolution and development of tiny cottages and barns. Each section is well illustrated with informative diagrams and sketches. The examples have obviously been carefully selected from a wide range of buildings scattered in obscure corners all over Wharfedale, Airedale and Ribblesdale in the south, to Swaledale and Wensleydale in the north. Even a person well acquainted with the Dales will most likely discover many buildings he never knew existed before.

In the closing chapter the author shows us how to look at buildings and tells us about the constructional features; how timber was used to form a building, what materials were used for the walls and floors, how the building was improved and enlarged, how the windows developed, why mullions were introduced; he mentions the carved doorways (a distinctive feature of the region), describes the roof construction and the craft of the thatcher and the slate striker (even listing some of the twenty or so names for the various sizes of slate). Finally he deals with the construction problems of the chimney and the traditions and functions of the fireplace.

Thirty years after the first publication of this book, it is reassuring to report that, unlike many other areas, most of the buildings mentioned still survive although generally they are in a poor condition. The main casualties have been the smaller buildings such as the cowsheds at Hurst, in Swaledale, which are now either derelict or abandoned. The barn at Barden Scale in Wharfedale was unfortunately dismantled ten years ago and moved to Shibden Hall Museum, near Halifax, where it later accidentally caught fire. The beautiful timbers of the aisled barn at Wigglesworth Hall have also suffered a similar fate. (The remaining listed buildings at Wigglesworth Hall and Hollin Hall Barn at Rathmell are now threatened by the proposed construction of a reservoir at Hellifield). More important, but less noticeable, has been the change in the way of life. With the introduction of modern farm machinery and improved transport during the past 20 years, many of the traditional crafts and farm practices (such as the systems of stinted pastures described on page 13) have disappeared, leaving buildings redundant or taken over for purposes alien to their original function. This is already having a detrimental effect on the appearance both of the landscape and the buildings, and it seems likely that many of our traditional farmsteads will either disappear or be altered beyond all recognition.

Again it is the smaller homesteads that are the most vulnerable for they are not protected by legislation. The cruck buildings, for example, at Drebley in Wharfedale (as far as we know the only ones existing now in the Dales) will deteriorate if they are not used. Some have already lost their roofs (e.g. the tiny cottage nearby at Club Nook); other similar barns both here and at Hurst in Swaledale now have corrugated sheet roofs in place of thatch, though sometimes part of the thatch remains under the sheeting (as at Water Gate Barn in Wharfedale). Thatching is no longer practised and, according to a recent survey, there is only one thatched building left in the Dales (2). However, despite their precarious existence, there are hopeful signs that many of these buildings will be preserved. There has never been a time when so many people have shown an interest in protecting them. Numerous surveys have been carried out (though surprisingly very few have been done in the Dales), and many new books have appeared — one of the best known being R. W. Brunskill's *Illustrated Handbook of Vernacular Architecture*. There has been official support, too, from the Royal Commission on Historical Monuments who have also published a major work — *English Vernacular Houses*. In the Dales, the opening of three new museums at Settle, Hawes and Grassington is yet another indication of the interest in the old customs and traditions. Furthermore, since 1952 the Dales have been designated as a National Park which gives the buildings additional status and protection.

One of the problems is to find new uses for buildings which are no longer used for their original purpose. Here the National Park has put forward some interesting proposals for the conservation and management of the Dales landscape. One proposal in particular — the conversion of redundant field barns to form 'stone tents' for holiday visitors — is an interesting idea and will not only protect the buildings but also ease the pressure of accommodating the increasing number of tourists.

The problem for the larger buildings is no longer demolition — there are too many people keen to purchase a house in the country — but 'over restoration' and the resulting loss of the characteristic features. The improvements carried out in nearly every home during the past couple of decades have changed the appearance and setting of the farmstead. The flagstones both inside and outside have disappeared under concrete; 'picture' windows have replaced mullion and sash windows, and other materials and ideas totally foreign to the area have been

(2) **History of Richmond and Swaledale**, by R. Fieldhouse and B. Jennings.

imported. William Morris, the founder of the Society for the Protection of Ancient Buildings, advised restorers to tamper as little as possible with the fabric, and mend and repair where it is required. Summersgill, near Burnsall (described on page 24), now no longer a farm, is a good example of how a farmstead can be adapted successfully to its new role.

This admirable introduction to Dales building, compiled in the period prior to the drastic alterations of the 1960s and 1970s, will be a useful guide to all those contemplating restoring old property. But perhaps one of its most valuable functions will be to encourage us to look more carefully and help us to understand the visual aspects of Dales buildings, picking out their characteristic features and the subtle changes that occur between one dale and the next.

— **JOHN MILLER**
June, 1979.

Author's Note

In the preparation of this small booklet I should like to thank the many good natured Dalesfolk who have offered me access to their homes and the value of their local knowledge.

My thanks are also due to my wife for many of the field sketches on which the illustrations have been based, and also to Dr. Arthur Raistrick for reading through my manuscript and for a number of suggestions which have been incorporated in the first chapter.

It is impossible in a work of this size to publish a complete account of the folk architecture of the Dales but it will, I hope, serve as an introduction to one of the most fascinating aspects of the Dales countryside.

No comprehensive account of Yorkshire folk architecture has yet been published but in the Bibliography I have indicated some of the more interesting works dealing with neighbouring districts and the subject in general which will prove helpful to those who wish to pursue the subject further.

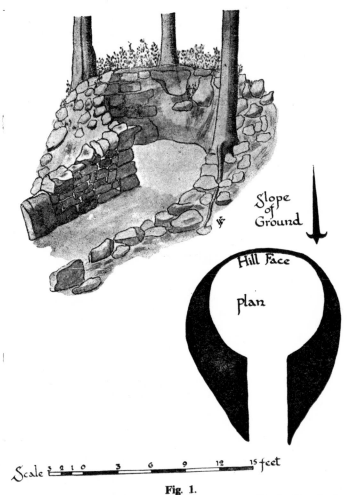

Slope of Ground

Hill Face

plan

Scale 3 2 1 0   3   6   9   12   15 feet

Fig. 1.
Foundations of circular Celtic dwellings in Grass Woods, Grassington.

1. The Homestead and its setting

THE sheltered valleys of the Yorkshire Dales, stretching up through bracken-covered slopes to the heather moors and limestone scars above, have been chosen as sites of habitation from the earliest times. Each succeeding race has left its mark; each has contributed to the speech, the customs, the lay-out of the villages and the architectural styles which to-day combine to produce that almost undefinable character we associate with the Yorkshire Dales. This is particularly true of the homesteads, the cottages bordering the village green, the halls and manor houses, the barns and the outbuildings. In these more remote parts of our island classical influence has had little effect and the buildings have assumed a character as purely local as the dialect of the people who dwell in them. They evolved according to the requirements of their owners. Each addition, each modification was made in accordance with changing economic and socal conditions. The Dalesman of old wasn't content to accept a ready-made house which the builder had designed. He knew what he required and he called in a mason to execute his demands. As a result the Dales homestead is in harmony with the country wherein it was born; an example of folk architecture in its purest form.

In Neolithic times the caves in the Great Scar Limestone served as shelters for the primitive peoples who occupied the Dales, where they tended their herds of goats, sheep and cattle. Remains of these animals and of the people themselves have been unearthed in Elbolton Cave, near Thorpe. Several of these caves, such as Dowkerbottom, near Kilnsey, and Victoria Cave, above Settle, were occupied even by the Iron Age peoples, but the more common habitation of these later settlers was the circular stone hut, traces of which may still be found in Grass Woods, near Grassington, in Deepdale above Yockenthwaite, on the western slopes of the Wharfe opposite Starbotton and in several other places in the Dales. Sufficient remains exist in some of the Grass Woods and Starbotton examples to afford us a fairly accurate picture of these primitive dwellings but thorough excavation is still needed to furnish the details.

The example figured from Grass Woods (Fig. 1) is typical of the group. They were dug out of the hillside to a depth of about five feet, a rock face often providing the rear wall, as at Starbotton. In front a wall of coarse rubble, from three to seven feet thick, completed a rough circle having an interior diameter of about ten feet. Of the nature of the roofing we cannot be certain but from the fact that in some cases the existing walls tend to taper inwards towards the top and from the mass of rubble collected in the centre of these huts we may deduce that the walls extended upwards to form the roof, so giving a bee-hive structure. A single passage opening, three feet wide and about seven feet long, served as doorway and window. Old manuscripts of the fifteenth century depict circular shepherds' huts in the Dales having vertical stone walls and a conical thatch of turf.

On the flat tops of the Great Scar Limestone at Lee Green, Grassington, Blue Scar, Arncliffe, Wedber Brow, opposite Gordale Scar, and on the summit of How Hill at Downholme in Swaledale are traces of early dwellings having a rectangular plan and often divided into a number of tiny compartments. The associated small enclosures bounded by walls of earth reinforced with rubble or, in the case of Wedber Brow, with megalithic limestone fences, probably housed the cattle at night. Running down the hillside from the hilltop settlements are long strips which were the arable land of the Celtic farmers and associated with these remains are dew ponds, burial mounds or tumuli and all the other evidence of a settled community.

Towards the end of the fifth and throughout the succeeding century, waves of invaders, loosely classed as Anglo-Saxons, occupied our Dales and drove the original Celtic inhabitants into the more remote uplands. These new-comers paid little attention either to the civilisation left by the Romans, which had little lasting effect in the Dales, or to the prevailing Celtic customs. They settled in the fertile valleys, establishing larger communal groups than the hamlets of their predecessors and these they called "tuns," a name which has been handed down to us in Airton, Carlton, Grassington and a host of other villages, many of which still have their Town-head, Town-end, or Town-top.

Generally each family was granted a "hide" of land consisting of the amount of arable land which a man could cultivate in a year with a full team of eight oxen, together with a proportionate share of pasture, meadow and common land. The unfree villager, or gebur, held only a quarter of a hide, or carucate as it came to be called later, and the outfit accompanying it was a pair of oxen, a cow and six sheep. Similarly a man with only one plough ox held only an eighth of a hide, later called a bovate or oxgang, whilst the cottar held about five acres which he was compelled to till with his spade and hoe.

The hide varied in size between eighty and a hundred and twenty acres, according to the nature of the land, but it was sufficiently standard to form a basis for taxation. In Upper Wharfedale, where the wealth of the villagers lay in pasture rather than in arable land, Raistrick and Chapman have indicated that the assessment was based on a rate of two carucates to one plough team instead of the usual four carucates per eight oxen. Addy has shewn that the size of a man's house was closely related to his holding and that, as oxen were indicative of a person's wealth, then the space required to house them was a convenient basis for taxation.

This classification prevailed for many centuries and in 1570 we learn from a survey made by the Crown's Commissioners that in Kirkby Malham "Henry Deane holds one tenement building with all houses belonging to the same with two bovates of land in the fields of Kyrkebye aforesaid with common and other things belonging. Robert Preston holds one cottage with a croft containing one acre and a-half with common and other appurtenances."

These holdings were not separate and compact farmsteads such as we know to-day. The village or "town" was a live social unit and each member of the community had his house with its adjoining farm buildings and a small field or croft stretching back from the road. This arrangement of "tofts and crofts" placed side by side along the main street through the village still prevails in most of the older Dales' villages, an excellent example being the tiny village of Colburn, near Richmond. Around the village, where all the homesteads of the inhabitants were gathered, lay the open arable fields which were cultivated in common by the associated partners. Usually there were two or three such fields, discernible in the names Eastfield, Westfield and Southfield still associated with many of our villages. In the long narrow valleys of Wensleydale and Wharfedale, Raistrick has pointed out that the villages are situated at the mid-point of two long fields ranged along the valley side, but in the much wider valleys of Airedale and Ribblesdale the fields are arranged in three groups around the village, as at Malham.

These fields were divided into a number of shots or fur-longs separated from each other by unploughed turf balks and the shots were in turn cut up into acre, half-acre, or quarter-acre strips. Each villager held a parcel of such strips in each field according to the number of oxen he maintained. In hilly country, such as the steep valley sides of Wharfedale and Swaledale, ploughing along the contours was a difficult operation and so, in some instances, the strips ran straight up the hillside at right angles to the contours. Such strips are usually associated with Celtic enclosures on the hill tops and probably originated in the Iron Age, although more field work is needed before the relationship between these two field systems can be exactly determined. In the majority of cases, however, the hill side was built up into flat terraces, varying in width from eight to sixteen yards, separated by a steep bank of earth or masonry. Where the slope was not excessive this was accomplished by repeatedly turning the sod downhill until the surface of the strip became level, but where the ground sloped steeply the face of the strip was often reinforced by rubble or dressed stone, as at Lawkland and Rathmell, and the strips became long level terraces, one above the other, whilst the belts between them were transformed into grassy banks often as high as nine or ten feet. These "lynchets", or "reins" as they are sometimes called, are common through-out the Dales. Excellent examples may be seen along the entire length of Wharfedale from Drebley to Buckden, be-tween Airton and Malham, in Airedale, and around Reeth and Downholme in Swaledale. This system of terrace cul-tivation, still universally employed in Mediterranean coun-tries and on the Himalayan slopes, was primarily a system of cultivation applied by the Saxons to all hilly arable land. The actual strips formed a basis for the sub-division of the land, but their chief function was to facilitate ploughing.

From seed time to harvest the arable fields were fenced against the livestock, but when the crops had been gathered in, the hayward removed the fences and the livestock of the village wandered freely over the fields. A similar system applied to the ings, still found in such names as Farnhill Ings, near Skipton, Bainbridge Ings near Hawes, and Fryer Ings near Bellerby. These were the meadows, situated in the low-lying land near a river or stream, and they were annually fenced off and apportioned out in lots or doles to be mown for hay. Above the arable and meadow land stretched the common pastures which formed an integral part of the village farm. They were jealously guarded by the privileged commoners against any intrusion by strangers and the agistment of strange cattle was strictly prohibited. Overstocking was also punished by the manorial court, for each common pasture was "stinted" or "limited" to a definite number of animals and to exceed this limit was to take an unfair advantage over the other villagers. In 1258 complaint was made to the King that the common pasture in Malham was being overstocked and he directed that the Sheriff of Yorkshire should have the pasture measured. As a result of this survey it was reported that "each bovate in Malgum is able to sustain 6 oxen and 6 cows with their young of 3 years, 4 mares with their young of three years, 200 sheeps, 5 she-goats, one sow with the young of one year, 4 geese and one gander." In the Court Rolls of the manor of Malham East for 1577 we find that, "The jurors say upon their oath that William Windsor has overstocked the pasture called the Lyngs with one mare and is therefor in mercy xii d; and that Ada Preston has trespassed within the fields of Malham aforesaid with one ox wrongfully straying beyond the Wetes Close, therefore in mercy iii s. iiii d."

This system of stinted common pastures is still maintained in many Dales' villages, such as Austwick, where shepherds are appointed annually to tend the sheep of the Austwick farmers from spring to autumn on the upland pastures. Austwick has three such pastures: Moughton, which is about 1,000 acres in extent; Ingleborough or Long Scar pasture, which is rather less, and Oxenber or Austwick Wood, whose size is variously estimated at between a hundred and three hundred acres. The grazing on each pasture is "stinted", Moughton, for example, being limited to six hundred "gaits" divided in varying proportions among a number of farms. A "gait" is the pasturage required for one sheep, four "gaits" is the pasturage of a cow, eight that of a horse, and ten that of a mare and foal. The shepherd is paid a certain price per gait, the price being determined at the annual meeting held in Austwick Parish Hall when the farmers vote for the shepherd they prefer, each farmer having a vote for every ten gaits allotted to his farm. The parishioners of Austwick, in addition to the three pastures, hold communal rights in Little Wood which is let to defray the expenses of mole catching and fencing of Oxenber. On the other two pastures mole catching is paid for by levy of a penny per gait on the farmers.

Survivals of Anglian field systems are not the only evidence remaining of their occupation of the Dales. Names such as "ton," an enclosure, were used equally by both the Anglian and the later Scandinavian settlers, but the terminations "ley," a meadow, "bridge," "croft," "den," "field," "ford," "ham," "hill," "wood" and "worth" are distinctively Anglian. The Scandinavian settlers of the late ninth century made an even greater contribution to the place-names of the Dales for, being pastoralists rather than agriculturalists, they occupied less fertile regions than the Anglo-Saxons. It is to the Vikings that we owe such names as "beck," "biggin," "by," "carr," "crook," "garth," "gate," "holme," "howe," "waithe," "lund," "mire," "nab," "rake," "scar," "storth," and "with." These were used equally by the Danish and Norse peoples but certain terminations are more specific. According to Goodall "thorpe" is distinctively Danish, whilst "cross," "ergh," "gill," "schole" and particularly "thwaite" characterise the Norse.

From the sixteenth century onwards the strips of the open fields were consolidated into separate holdings and the common pastures were enclosed. Separate farmsteads replaced the communal system which had prevailed for so many centuries and the pattern of the Dales gradually assumed its present form. But the old names still survive. Here and there the gaited pastures are still let annually and the villages themselves still retain their old character. Houses and barns line the main street as they did of old and in many cases the farmer still lives within the village, going out daily to his fields. Isolated laithes were built to shelter the cattle and store the crops of the more remote fields but the Dales' populace is to a great extent concentrated within the villages.

2. Cottage and Barn

AMONG farmers everywhere traditional methods die hard and, in the remote parts of the Yorkshire Dales, buildings still retain systems of construction and nomenclature which have been handed down almost unchanged from the early Norse and Danish settlers. Both peoples adopted the practice of having permanent winter houses in the sheltered valleys and moving with their families and livestock to the upland pastures during the summer months when they lived in crude shelters, or booths, of wattle and thatch. Of these summer houses we have little evidence but such names as Summerside, Summersgill and Summerlodge bear witness to the existence of a similar annual transhumance from the valleys to the high pastures in our own Dales. The custom is still widespread in the upland regions of the Alps, the cis-Himalayan tract and in Norway where the temporary summer settlements are known as *saeters,* a name which in its Anglo-Saxon form *sett,* a fold or cattle-stall, may be traced in such Dales' place-names as Appersett, Burtersett and Countersett. The winter house has had far less nominal influence but we have a Winterscales as well as a Summerscales, "scale" being derived from the Norse "skali," meaning a shepherd's hut.

An interesting survival of transhumance in the Yorkshire Dales is provided by the "cow clubs" of Castle Bolton and Preston-under-Scar where anyone renting land in the village is allowed to feed from one to five cows on the upland "gaited" pastures. These small farmers combine to form a club which employs a "rabbit man" to catch the rabbits and a "by-law man" who repairs the walls and brings the cattle to the milking place. Night and morning from the middle of May to the middle of September the owners climb up the fellside to milk their cattle in the open.

The buildings which approximate most closely to the summer booths of our Nordic ancestors are the tiny cow byres scattered throughout the remote uplands around Hurst, near Reeth. These are simple rectangular structures with coarse rubble walls replacing the wattle of old

Primitive Cowshed
HURST

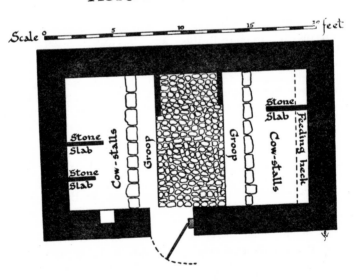

Fig. 2. Upland cowshed, Hurst, Swaledale.

and a roof of turf or ling thatch resting on undressed branches. The example figured is typical of the group (Fig. 2). Twenty-two feet long and a little over thirteen feet wide, it is entered by a doorway placed about in the middle of one side. There are no windows and the door-ways provided the only illumination. Inside, a cobbled pathway, five feet wide, divides the building into two parts and at the remote end of this pathway two upright stone slabs form a crude fireplace. Adjoining this cobbled path on each side are narrow drainage channels, or groops, which separate the path from the cow stalls. The latter afford only the minimum accommodation for the cattle which are separated from each other by vertical stone slabs.

The winter house was a more substantial structure built on "crucks" or "forks." Two pairs of bent trees, or more commonly, trees sawn down the middle, were set up on the ground and united at their apexes by a ridge tree. Each pair of crucks was strengthened by a tie-beam and the cruck feet were often raised on stone pedestals, or stylobats, to preserve them. The sloping walls of such a building res-tricted the living space within the house and the next evolutionary step was to make the walls vertical. This was accomplished by extending the tie-beams outwardly until they became equal in length to the base of the arch formed by the crucks (Fig. 3). On the ends of these extended tie-beams long beams, known as "pans," were laid, the rafters stretching from these to the ridge-tree. Finally a side wall was built from the ground up to the pan which thereby rested on top of the wall.

Originally the upper part of the walls was of wattle rest-ing on a low foundation wall of stone rubble and in the compotus for the year 1454 rendered by John Dytton, vicar of Kirkby Malham, to the Abbey of Dereham, an interest-ing account is given of the actual construction of such a dwelling. The vicar "paid for thakke bought of T. Rakys, and watlyng and thakkyng 2 houses entirely, viz., his said dwelling house in Avrton and the barn of the same house, 18/4d. Also for drink given to the carpenters and for basyng the said houses, that is to say, for laying great stones under the foot of the Crokk, 4d." The house of Thomas Rakys in Airton was, then, built on crucks supported on "great stones" and its walls were of rubble and wattle. Of the nature of the "thakkyng" we have no record but it was most probably of ling or turf laid on closely spaced rafters.

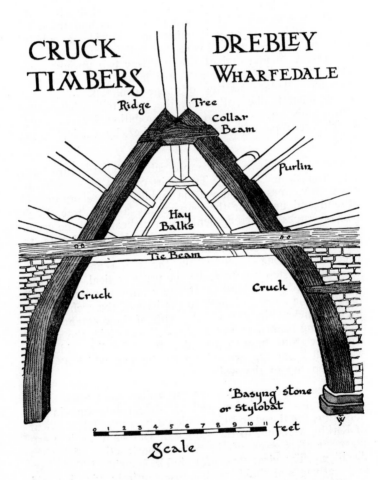

Fig 3. Cruck framework of a barn at Drebley, Wharfedale.

Simple cruck buildings survived in the more isolated parts of the Dales until the present century, particularly in the barns where obsolete methods lingered long after they had been abandoned in the houses themselves. Excellent examples may still be found in the districts around Barden and Drebley (Fig. 4), and in the neighbourhood of Bolton-by-Bowland, where, in over a thousand years, the replacement of wattle by rubble walling has been the only important change.

The barn at Barden Scale, which is unfortunately tumbling into ruin, has two pairs of crucks dividing it into three areas known as "bays." The length of the bay in this case varies from eleven to seventeen and a-half feet, but it is more usually between fourteen and sixteen feet. The seventeenth century barn at East Riddlesden, for instance, has eight bays, each approximately fourteen feet in length, whilst the two barns at Drebley have sixteen-feet bays, and Addy has put forward the suggestion that this was the space required for four oxen. Since the dwelling house, barn and mistal were often grouped under the same roof, as we shall see when we examine a Dales' "coit," the application of the bay as a unit of measurement was extended to buildings in general, and in old records references to "a house of 3 bays" or "a barn of 4 bays" are quite common. In support of this contention Addy quotes Palladius who, in giving directions about building a Roman ox-house in the year 210 A.D., says, "eight feet are more than sufficient standing room for each pair of oxen," and the Welsh Laws which state that oxen were eight feet in the field yoke and sixteen feet in the long yoke, that is, in a team of four. As we have seen, teams of four oxen were commonly employed in Saxon times and since they were housed in the stalls as a team it is highly probable that the length of a bay did originate in this manner.

In the barn at Barden Scale (Fig. 4) the longest bay serves as the shippons, or cow-stalls, housing six cattle in its seventeen and a-half feet. In the middle of the south side is a pair of large barn doors, raised above the level of the side wall to allow the entry of loaded corn or hay waggons, and in a corresponding position in the north wall is a smaller "winnowing door." The floorspace between these two sets of doors is the threshing-stead, for here the corn was threshed with a flail and the grain was winnowed from the chaff. On a suitably breezy day the farmer opened both sets of doors and as he gently agitated the mixture

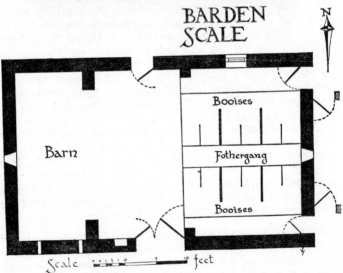

Fig 4. The old barn at Barden Scale, Wharfedale.

of corn and chaff in a shallow winnowing scoop the draught carried away the lighter chaff whilst the heavier grain dropped almost vertically down in a pile close to his feet.

A little further up Wharfedale at Club Nook is a tiny cottage, occupied up to the end of last century, which displays a simplicity of structure comparable to the barn at Barden (Fig. 5). This is a dwelling of two short bays, the whole measuring only twenty-two feet by thirteen and a-half feet. In its present form it is divided into two unequal parts, a pantry seven feet wide and a living room, the floor of which is six inches lower than that of the pantry. Over the living room is a floor terminating on the dividing wall to provide a loft, open at one end, which was used as a bedroom. Entrance to the loft is gained by means of a wooden ladder resting on two stone steps built against the end wall. The dividing wall and the loft are certainly not part of the original structure for the tie-beam of the central pair of crucks with a ridge-pole is of particular interest in view of the repeated references in the Welsh Laws of the twelfth and thirteenth centuries to these same three timbers. The Dimetian Code stipulated that "if timber be cut in a person's wood without his permission other than the three timbers which are free for a builder on field-land," then certain fees had to be paid. Again it is stated that "three timbers which each builder upon field-land should have from the owner of the wood, whether the woodman will it or not, a ridge-piece and two roof-forks." These are the timbers employed in the timber structure of Club Nook cottage and they no doubt represent a very ancient building tradition. The entrance door and nearby window have a long wooden lintel above, on which rests a double course of stone slates projecting about six inches from the wall in the form of a drip-stone. The wall here is thinner than the remainder of the building and it seems probable that the space now occupied by the door and window was at one time a larger doorway. An almost identical door and window exists, however, in the barn at Water Gate on the opposite bank of the river, occupying the normal position of the winnowing door (Fig. 13).

The cottage as it now stands is identical, apart from the position of the doorway, with the *croglofft* dwellings described by Peate as characteristic of Welsh cottages. The following Welsh examples emphasise the marked similarity. "The more common type of cottage is a low straw-thatched stone building with two rooms downstairs, one being a large

CLUB NOOK COTTAGE
Drebley

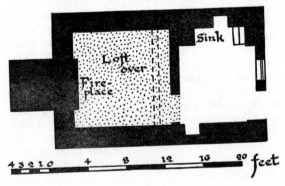

Fig. 5. Cruck framed cottage, Drebley, Wharfedale.

roomy kitchen where all the cooking, eating and washing is done, and where as a rule there is a bed as well. The other room is generally very small and almost always damp. Over these two rooms there is a loft, generally approached by a ladder with the roof coming down to the floor." Again, in Monmouthshire, a cottage at Raglan "had a very good living room, twelve feet by ten feet, with a small back scullery. The bedroom was about two feet lower than the living room and four feet by ten feet. Over this was a small apartment in the roof. There were no stairs to the roof apartment, the ascent being made from the living room by chairbacks or a small ladder."

Originally the cottage at Club Nook was a single room open to the rafters. It may have had a partition where the dividing wall now stands but more probably a dresser, or similar piece of furniture, served to divide the room into two parts. The most striking feature is the massive stone chimney situated at the gable end oppsite the doorway where it projects from the wall for a distance of four and a-half feet, and rises to a height of several feet above the ridge of the roof. No doubt this type of chimney was introduced to safeguard the thatched roof from catching fire, for this was one of the greatest dangers in the past and contributed largely to the change from thatch to stone slates.

3. The Long House or "Coit"

THE cottage of one or two bays proved hopelessly inadequate and it was extended by the addition of further bays or by building extra rooms either at the ends or sides. These additional rooms were known as "outshots" or "outshuts," Norse "skot"—a part of a building shut off from the rest. The addition of extra bays gave rise to a long house with the barn and cow shed or mistal often under the same roof. Where access to the barn could be gained by a doorway leading direct from the house it was known as a "cote" or "coit" and, although survivals of this type are now somewhat rare, the long house with a dividing wall between the house and barn is one of the typical arrangements in our Dales' farmsteads.

An excellent example of a sixteenth century stone "coit," complete with toft and croft of four or five acres, may still be seen at Summersgill on the roadside between Burnsall and Appletreewick (Fig. 6). The arrangement of the rooms within the house is almost identical with that in the old Norse house which had a women's apartment or chamber, a fire-house or house-place and a pantry or buttery. The main door leads direct into the house-place which originally was the only room with a fire and consequently was the common room, serving as kitchen, dining room and sitting room. The fireplace is in the centre of the building and is screened from the draughts by a projecting "speer." From the house-place one door behind the speer, now walled up, led into the barn, thus allowing the farmer to visit his cattle without having to go outside in inclement weather, whilst a second led to the bower or women's apartment. The bower gradually lost its original significance and ultimately became the parlour. The buttery at Summersgill is an outshot placed at the end of the building adjoining the bower. At some later period a stone staircase was built here thus reducing the size of the buttery and obscuring two of its windows which were walled up. Entry to the upper rooms was originally gained

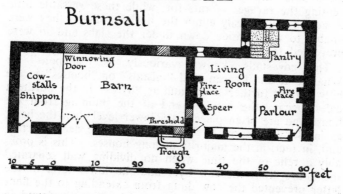

Fig. 6. A typical stone "Coit", Summersgill, Burnsall.

by means of a wooden ladder such as the one in use at Club Nook and in many of the cottages of the Yorkshire Wolds.

Of particular interest is the walled-up doorway adjoining that leading into the house-place. At a very early date this was the main entrance to the whole building, access to the house being gained via the doorway behind the speer. In the opposite wall is another walled-up doorway, the original winnowing door, and the space between was the threshing floor. As Addy has pointed out with regard to a similar building at Fulwood, near Sheffield, this main doorway led directly on to what was literally the "threshold" in the truest sense of the word. The threshold separated the house from the barn with its large barn doors and winnowing door of later date. Even this second winnowing door has now been walled up, either because the introduction of the winnowing fan or the conversion of arable land into pasture rendered it obsolete. In the barn the hay or corn harvest was stored, but where the available room was inadequate to house the whole of the harvest, stacks were built outside in a walled enclosure known as the "stack-garth," norse — *stakk,* stacks, and *gard,* an enclosure. These were built on upright stone blocks surmounted by flat stone slabs on which rested the stack base of timber and brushwood. This support, known as a "brandrey," Anglo-Saxon *brandreth,* a support, served the double purpose of keeping the stack-base dry and preventing the ravages of rats for, while these versatile little creatures could easily climb the upright pillars, they were unable to walk upside down under the slabs and so were prevented from reaching the grain.

The cow-stalls, known variously as "shippons" in Wharfedale and Craven, and "mistals" or "booises" in the hilly regions further south, and as "byres" in the northern dales, occupy the opposite end of the building from the house and are often placed at a lower level than the barn, as in Bombey Barn, Drebley, Wood House near Marrick and, in fact, in the majority of long houses. This is probably a relic of the time when no dividing wall separated the house from the cow byre and the lower level of the latter prevented the cow dung from extending to the floor of the living room. Such a system is generally found in India to-day where peasant and cattle share the same building.

A separate doorway leads direct on to the "causey" adjoining the end of the byre. It leads, too, into one of our richest sources of pure dialect, for the names still employed are almost wholly of direct Scandinavian or Anglo-Saxon origin. Separating the passage from the "booises" is a channel, the "groop," to collect the manure and the booises themselves, unlike the primitive Hurst cowsheds, are divided by wooden "skell-booises" in place of the upright stone slabs. The cows are "sealed" in the booises by a sealing rope, made by the country rope makers such as the one at Hawes, and this is attached to an iron ring, or "framble," which slides up and down a vertical wooden post, the "booise-stake" or "stang," secured to the side of the skell-booise. At the edge of the booise floor, or 'settle-gang," is a wooden beam, the "settle-tree," which holds up the bedding and prevents it from sliding into the groop. According to Crump, at one time this was not fixed but was free to move on chains so that its position could be adjusted.

At the head of each booise is a feeding rack, or "heck," to hold the fodder and this is filled by the farmer from a pathway known as the "fodder-em" or "fothergang" which at Summersgill coincides with the threshing stead but is usually a separate passage dividing the mistal from the barn. In the wall of such old mistals as Summersgill one may often find a number of recesses where the farmer stores his cattle medicine, a horn for administering it, and a miscellaneous assortment of oddments needed for the welfare of his stock. Some of the larger recesses house the milking pails or piggins from which the milk is poured into the larger churns which formerly were cooled in the large stone trough found in all the older farmyards. At East Riddlesden two of these recesses are cusped, a feature which I have only noticed in three other instances, all in the parish of Halifax. A manure shoot is also usually pro- vided in the same end wall and again East Riddlesden affords a unique example, for the wooden doors covering this aperture slide between two long grooved stones. Within the barn all is dim, it has an air of reverend solemnity, and the only source of light is a series of narrow slits or trian- gular openings, known as "lowp hoils" or "laap hoils," which were intended for ventilation rather than illumin- ation.

4.   The Stone House

THE dominant building material in the South Pennine area was, for many centuries, timber and wattle. Ecclesiastical buildings and the homes of the more important gentry were, however, built of stone, and in Markenfield Hall, near Ripon, Nappa Hall, near Askrigg, and Farnhill Hall, near Kildwick, we have excellent examples of fourteenth and fifteenth century houses still preserving their original lay-out, although Farnhill has been considerably modernised. Calton Hall, in Malhamdale, has retained slight vestiges of its original structure, which indicate that it was a stone house of the same type. The most striking feature of these old stone houses is the massive square tower, a survival from an earlier period when it comprised the entire living accommodation and provided a measure of defence which long remained necessary in the North country. Bolling Hall, near Bradford, has such a tower, which Kitson ascribes to the middle of the fourteenth century, and Yanwath Tower, Westmorland, which was built in 1325, also has a tower very similar to that of Nappa.

According to Leland, writing in 1538, Nappa Hall was built by Thomas Metcalfe, whose father, James, had covered himself with glory at Agincourt in 1415. This second Metcalfe, he says, "waxed rich and builded the two faire towers" which are connected by the great hall. Assuming that Leland is correct, then the entire house dates from the middle of the fifteenth century. The massive western tower is, however, a self-contained dwelling almost identical with Bolling and Yanwath and it is highly probable that Thomas Metcalfe may have made alterations to this part of the house when he added the hall and lower eastern tower in the years 1450 to 1459. That a house did exist earlier is shewn by Leland's statement that there was "but a cotage or little better house ontille Thomas Metcalfe began then to build," and this was "communely caullid 'No castel'." The tower contains a kitchen and pantry on the ground floor with a circular stone newel staircase leading to the first floor which is also divided into

Fig. 7. Nappa Hall, near Askrigg, Wensleydale.

two rooms. The larger of these was panelled in oak and had a plaster frieze, a fragment of which still remains. The smaller room was probably a chapel as it has what appears to be a stone piscina. The room above in that case would be the solar, or retiring room, of the lord of the manor, whilst the top floor may have been a chamber or servants' quarters. This plan is identical with that of the typical Norman keep and indicates the necessity of a defensive structure as a protection against the marauding Scots.

In 1459 Nappa Hall took on a new form in keeping with the current ideas of comfort and privacy. A tower of two storeys in the eastern wing was divided from the earlier western tower by a large hall measuring forty-four feet by twenty-three feet. The entrance to the hall was screened off by wooden screens, now replaced by a stone wall, which separated the hall from the entrance passage and above this was the minstrels' gallery (Fig. 7). Two mullioned windows, with drip-stones terminating in stone masks, provided light for the hall which was originally open to the rafters. These windows are almost identical with the late fifteenth century examples in the guest house of Abingdon Abbey in Berkshire, and have similar protecting iron grilles. Ambler suggests that the great fireplace, which was the most important feature of these old halls, was situated in the north wall. The east tower was the bower, or women's apartment, and also included the kitchen and buttery, now known as the "wine cellar." The more imposing western tower then became the solar, or retiring room for the menfolk. Here at Nappa we have a perfect example of the fourteenth and fifteenth century stone house surviving almost unchanged, although additions in the form of a south-east wing were made in the seventeenth century. The tower at Yanwath had a similar hall and kitchen added to the original tower.

Equally interesting is the hall at Hipswell, near Richmond, probably built by Alan Fulthorpe about 1484, and crenellated like Nappa and Farnhill. This has a central porch tower in the middle of the south wall leading into the hall on the east side and the bower and kitchen on the west. This follows the traditional pattern, for the passage between the front and back doors usually divided the hall from the bower. It originated as a wooden screen or partition, with two doorways, which protected the hall from draught and was known as the "screens passage." Above it was often placed the so-called "minstrels' gallery," as at Nappa Hall. In the smaller houses the screen extends for only a short distance into the room when it is known as a "speer." A wooden bench is usually fitted on the inside of the speer, as at Blackburn Hall, Grinton, whilst a shelf on the top holds the pots and dishes.

An unusual passage survives at Barden Scale in Wharfedale. The front door is a double barn-like door affording access to a wide passage dividing the house into two parts. On the right are the peat house and kitchen, complete with bakstone. On the left a doorway leads into the pantry, with its fine old polished oak meal ark, and so to the parlour, still richly provided with well carved oak chests and dressers.

At the end of the hall opposite the screens was a dais or raised platform where the master of the house sat and dined with his family. The servants dined at a long table arranged down the middle of the room and presided over by the senior labourer, the remainder occupying chairs in order of seniority; an order jealously preserved. In the fifteenth century the custom was instituted of illuminating the high table by means of a bay window. This is rare in Yorkshire but Hipswell boasts an excellent example which illuminates both the hall and the room above and bears the cross moline of the Fulthorpes. The hall was enclosed by handsome gardens and terraces bounded by a moat, and some idea of the extent of the outbuildings may be gained from the extensive foundations still remaining. To the north is the "Chapel Garth," and Mr. Metcalfe, the stalwart old farmer at Hipswell, informs me that in dry weather the entire foundations of the chapel may be traced by the parched grass. A private chapel was provided in many of the old manor halls for the lord of the manor and his household.

These early stone buildings such as Nappa and Farnhill retained the general plan of the fortified Norman keep in their massive towers but in the provision of a great hall and buttery on the ground floor they displayed features which were developed from the manor house. The main room in both the hall and the manor house was the hall itself, and in the earlier houses it was the only room of any importance. A solar at one end and a kitchen and bower at the other were the only additional rooms apart from the chapel. A few of these early manor houses have survived as chapels long after they ceased to serve their original purpose. Addy has described such an example at Padley Chapel in Derbyshire, and in St. Ann's Chapel at Colburn, near Richmond, we have in the Dales a building which probably served as a thirteenth or four-teenth-century manor house. This is a simple rectangular two-storeyed structure measuring forty-eight feet by twenty-three feet and now serving as cow-stalls and granary. It runs north and south and the entire illumination was formerly provided by a window in each gable. The upper floor, which included chapel and hall, was reached by an external staircase, as it still is, and it has a fireplace in the east wall. No doubt the ground floor served as storeroom and servants' quarters, but little of the original arrangement can be traced apart from the round-headed doorway in the east wall.

The earliest Norman domestic buildings, such as the manor hall of Boothby Pagnell near Grantham, and the so-called "Jews' Houses" of Lincoln and Bury St. Edmunds, are almost identical in lay-out with the chapel of St. Ann. In all these cases the living rooms were on the upper floor where the fireplace occupied a position towards the centre of one side wall. A wooden partition may have divided the room into two parts, the larger one serving as the hall and the smaller one as the bower. The hall probably also served as kitchen, for no definite cooking place can be recognised. Professor Hamilton Thompson has suggested the "cooking may have been been done in the cellar, but the only outlet for smoke was through the doorway, and it is very doubtful whether the ground floor was generally used for any other purpose than that of cellarage." It is possible that unless the cooking was done in the hall the kitchen may have been housed in a separate building. The monastic kitchen of Glastonbury and the kitchens of Raby Castle and Stokesay Castle were so isolated and it may have been a general practice. Otherwise the function of the ground floor is something of a problem. In the town houses of Lincoln and elsewhere it would provide storage. This may also be true of such country houses as Colburn where it could also have been used to accommodate the servants and labourers. In some cases the cellar or ground floor roof was vaulted and we still have an example in the Dales at Well Hall, two miles north of Tanfield. This building has been considerably modernised but it still retains the vaulted cellar built by Ralph Neville in 1342.

In Scolland's Hall, Yorkshire boasts one of the earliest examples of Norman domestic architecture in the country. Situated in the south-east angle of the wall of Richmond Castle, it was probably built by Alan, Earl of Brittany

(1071-1089) but it was apparently named after Scolland, Lord of Bedale, who was senschal to a later Earl Alan (1137-1146). The upper floor, which housed the hall and was reached by an external staircase, has gone but, as Miss Margaret Wood has pointed out, the remaining joist holes show "how little the builders cared for the parallel, the beams apparently slanting across the building as in William II's hall at Westminster." There is a newel stair, partially blocked, in the north-west angle, but only the foundations of the external hall staircase remain.   Of the original features the two-light windows and a doorway with jamb-shafts and Corinthianesque capitals in the hall and the loops in the south wall of the basement may still be seen. Some herring-bone masonry occurs in the north and west walls and there are the remains of a twelfth-century cor-bel table on the south wall. To the east is the original solar, much altered in the thirteenth century, whilst to the west are offices built in the early twelfth century.

The halls of Nappa and Hipswell and the manor house at Colburn provide us with excellent examples of the three main trends in mediaeval domestic stone buildings. The western tower of Nappa with ground floor kitchen, first floor hall and chapel and second floor solar represents the defensive Pele-tower type, characterising the north country and illustrating the influence of the Norman keep. Hips-well illustrates the second type, consisting of a hall with bower and kitchen on the ground floor, the two being separated by the "screens passage." The two upper rooms were the chambers or maybe one of them served as a solar. This was the forerunner of all subsequent stone houses built in the sixteenth and seventeenth centuries when a balancing room was added at the end of the hall opposite the bower. A certain measure of defence was provided by an encircling moat. St. Ann's Chapel at Col-burn affords an example of the third type wherein the hall and bower were situated on the first floor which was reached by an external staircase.

The early development of these house types is well illustrated by the fine old moated manor house of Mar-kenfield to the south of Ripon. This well preserved four-teenth-century homestead has been described and illus-trated in many works and the following account is based on the work of Professor Hamilton Thompson. It was in 1310 that John de Merkingfield, a wealthy landowner who was in holy orders, a clerk in the King's service and a canon of York, obtained a licence to crenellate, and the earliest part dates from a little after that time. This consists of an L-shaped block which includes the hall. This is on the first floor and was reached by an outer staircase. At the east end of the hall, where the high table was situated, a doorway leads into the bower and to the rooms in the three-storeyed wing. The rooms in this wing include the great chamber, with its fine fireplace in the east wall, a chaplain's room and chapel complete with piscina, and a small garderobe which projects near the north-east corner. The latter had an outlet to the moat similar to that which may be seen in Skipton Castle. The other rooms in this wing were probably used as guest chambers and household offices, the various floors being reached from a turret staircase similar to that at Nappa, which leads on to the roof. The kitchens were situated on the ground floor beneath the hall.

The mediaeval family lived communally in the great hall, and in the earliest stone houses the master was the only one assured of any privacy. This desire for additional seclusion was one of the major factors in the subsequent development of the house and Markenfield had a number of rooms in addition to those required by the lord. Towards the end of the sixteenth century the Dales, in common with the rest of England, experienced a period of increased prosperity. Highways were improved, bridges were built or repaired and the farmers were thus enabled to readily market their surplus produce, particularly wool. The manorial system was breaking down, land was enclosed, sheep farming was fostered on the upland pastures and a class of freeholder was established who lived on the produce of his land and grew rich on the sale of wool in distant markets. The miserable homestead built on cruck, with its wattled walls and ling thatched roof was no longer sufficient and a spate of building in stone resulted. Everywhere throughout the Dales we can still see the sturdy dwellings built at the end of the sixteenth and in the early part of the seventeenth centuries with the initials of their proud owners and the date of erection carved on the ornate lintel above the door. Many were merely translations into stone of the earlier timber and wattle structures but others developed a structural plan characteristic of the period and the new medium. They still retained the central hall with the bower at one end and the solar at the other but more rooms were added in the nature of outshuts. Stone slates, or thakstones, replaced the ling thatch and the tiny windows scattered irregularly over the wall face were replaced by a symmetrical arrangement of mullioned windows having drip-stones with ornate terminations. Glass was cheaper and, as money was more plentiful among the new house-builders, a fashion arose of making the windows as large as possible, especially in the hall.

The seventeenth-century halls of these yeomen consisted essentially of a large central room, the "house-body" or "fire-house," with wings at each end, one of which contained the parlour and store-rooms whilst the other was occupied by the kitchen, buttery, pantry and dairy. In some cases the symmetry is less marked. Blackburn Hall at Grinton has the usual house-body but only one wing, and the parlour and kitchen are both in this wing.

The halls of the yeoman farmers of the sixteenth and seventeenth centuries were more pretentious than the earlier homesteads yet the interior furnishings, judged by modern standards, were still only meagre. There were no carpets, very little in the way of table linen, hardly any glass or crockery and no knives or forks. Some idea of the furnishings of these old halls may be gleaned from the wills of their owners. All the cooking was done in the hall, or house-body, where we find the "spitts, drippinge pann and broylinge irons," brass mortars, chafing dishes, ladles, striking knives, chopping bills, brandreth and other culinary utenils. Here, too, was the long oak table and the chairs or benches on which the farm workers sat whilst the master of the house and his family dined at a smaller table in front of the fire. An oak cupboard held the pewter comprising the dishes, porringers, flagons and doublers. The last-named were dishes, hollowed on both sides so that they may be turned over to hold a second course.

The parlour usually served as a bedroom, being fitted with a bed and bedclothes as well as odd chests and tables. The upstairs rooms held beds and chests but also served as storerooms for a miscellaneous assortment of farming and weaving appliances. The kitchen was little more than a dairy but it usually housed the solid meal ark in which the oatmeal was stored. Here, too, were the cheese vats, butter bowls, butter prints and churns in addition to the "masker" and "galker" for brewing, the "powdringe kit" in which beef was salted and the "knade kit" wherein oatmeal was mixed with water in the preparation of oatcake.

The interior woodwork of these seventeenth-century halls achieved a standard of craftsmanship which has never

BOMBEY BARN
DREBLEY

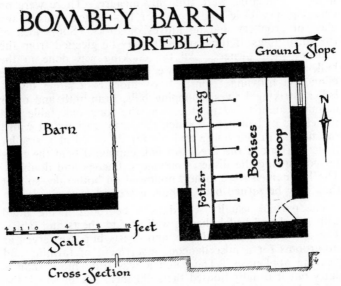

Fig. 8.   Bombey Barn, Drebley, Wharfedale.

been equalled since. Rich black oak panelling covered the walls of the house body and some of the other rooms, adzed oak joists supported the pegged floors whilst the staircases, with their turned balusters and newels, provide that delight which arises from workmanship born of pride. The early seventeenth-century homestead of Bolton Peel, near Bolton-by-Bowland, still retains its original woodwork almost complete. The doors are of oak boards fitted with wooden latches and they still swing as freely as they did three hundred years ago. During the same period ornamental plasterwork made its appearance. Panels over the fireplaces, friezes and ceilings were enriched with a variety of plaster cast motifs many of which still remain. Bare as the seventeenth-century house may seem to-day it was a far more comfortable dwelling than the early peel-like tower of Norman times. Such fittings as were provided were well made and amply fitted their purpose; a sure test of all that is good in craftsmanship.

The development in the barn buildings followed similar lines to the transition from wood to stone houses. We have already noticed that the old Norse barn, from which our earliest examples were derived, was a simple rectangular building with great barn doors placed centrally on one side facing a smaller winnowing door in the opposite wall and with the shippons or mistals at one end where they were entered by a separate door. The old barns at Drebley, in Wharfedale, are of this type, the only relief being provided by a simple porch.

The first stage in the subsequent development was the addition of an outshut at the mistal end of the barn, thus affording increased accommodation for the cattle, as at Sulber Laithe, near Thorlby, or Bombey Barn, near Barden (Fig. 8). This demand for extra mistals probably arose owing to the change from arable land to pasture which took place during this period. Then followed the addition of a second outshut on the other side of the barn doors which was used as a calf house. And so finally the roof was extended along the entire length of one side with the great barn doors recessed in a porch from which access could often be gained by side doors to the calf house on one side and the mistals on the other. As a result of this change the front wall was considerably reduced in height and loaded waggons were unable to enter the porch. To overcome this one of three alternatives was adopted; either the roof of the porch was raised, as at Barden Scale, or a gabled porch was built,

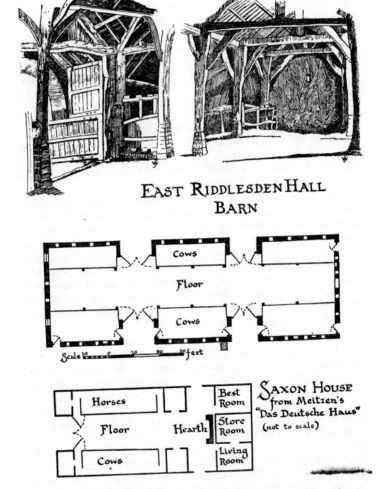

EAST RIDDLESDEN HALL
BARN

Fig. 9. East Riddlesden Hall Barn, near Keighley, with a plan
of a Saxon house for comparison.

as at East Riddlesden, or the entrance to the barn was unroofed.

By the addition of outshuts along the entire length of both front and back walls a basilical structure, divided into nave and aisles, would result and this is the form of the larger barns such as Wigglesworth Hall, Bolton Abbey and East Riddlesden (Fig. 9). But these larger barns have a fundamentally different interior arrangement for the cattle stalls. Instead of being at one end they are placed along the aisles and the cattle face inwards towards the barn floor. This is almost identical with the Saxon and Friesian house described by August Meitzen in his book, "Das deutsche Hause in seinen volksthumlichen Formen," from which I quote the following translation by Addy :—

"Its ground plan is that of a basilica with nave and aisles. The middle always forms the so-called 'floor' which is entered at the gable end through a large gate, and which goes through the whole house as far as the dwelling rooms at the end . . . In the forms of the Friesian and Saxon house generally in use the horses and cows are always so placed on both sides of the 'floor' that they are foddered from it. Over the 'floor,' over the cattle stalls and over all the other rooms up to the ridge of the roof the corn harvest and hay harvest are stored on boards and poles laid between the joists. In the Saxon house the back ground of the 'floor' ends in a low hearth on both sides of which are the bedsteads of the family arranged in a kind of narrow and rather high cupboards, whilst over against them, and near them, the men-servants sleep over the horses and the maids over the cows."

The use of one end of the Saxon barn as a dwelling house is of considerable interest for in many of the Dales' barns, such as Appletreewick Low Hall, one end bay is arranged like a small house with a flight of outside stairs leading to the upper floor and there is ample evidence to show that formerly the farm labourers slept over the cattle. In the Richmond wills of the sixteenth century there are frequent references to bedding in the ox-house such as the following:—

1556 In the oxen house viij coverletts, iij blankets, xiijs. iijd.

1567 Servannts bedes in the oxhouse, iiijs. iiijd.

1569 In the cowe house, iij old coverlets, a paire blanckets, a paire sheits, a matteras, and a bolster xs.

The fact that bedsteads are not mentioned indicates that the servants slept on mattresses placed directly on the boards and there are people still in the Dales who remember farm labourers sleeping on a pile of hay on the boards above the cattle. Until quite recently the Irish labourers, who came over in large numbers for the haymaking season, adopted a similar practice.

And so we see that the arrangement of the Saxon house is almost identical with that of our larger barns except for the position of the main entrance, and it seems possible that whereas the long house with shippons at one end is of Nordic origin the larger barn was derived from the Saxon equivalent. It may be, of course, that the Saxon house itself was originally a simple rectangular structure to which outshuts were added along each side.

The Dales' farmstead is compact; barn, shippons, calf-boxes, horse-stalls and even the house are often included under the same roof. The arrangement of a disconnected group of buildings around a central farmyard, so characteristic of East Yorkshire and the lower stretches of the Dales, is rare in the higher reaches of the rivers. Occasionally, especially in Swaledale and Wensleydale, stone hen-cotes, granaries and cart sheds may be found. In lower Swaledale, too, the wheel-houses, often with their gearing removed, still remain to remind us of the change from a farming system entirely reliant on manual labour to one which made greater use of animal power. Their giant cobweb-covered power wheels turn no longer for the petrol engine has rendered them useless. Even in the Dales horse-driven chaff cutters and horse-drawn ploughs are to-day giving way to the petrol engine and the tractor.

The wheel-house is an octagonal structure abutting on the barn to which it was added at the end of the eighteenth or in the early part of the nineteenth century. The first threshing mill was built in 1790, but the numbers were greatly increased by the end of the century. Winnowing fans, or "cloths," which replaced the more natural draught of the threshing-stead, gave way to the box winnowing machines even earlier and they too needed power for their operation. So the wheel house was built. Within this octagonal building a massive wooden-toothed wheel supported on a stout vertical wooden axle was turned by a pair of horses plodding in a monotonous circle. A smaller wooden-toothed gearwheel converted the horizontal rotation to a vertical rotation capable of driving the chaff cutter, winnowing machine, threshing machine or turnip

40

chopper.   An excellent example is still preserved in a farmstead at Hudswell, near Richmond.

Another outbuilding of some interest may be found in association with the farms around Barden and Drebley, which was at one time an important potato growing district. The crops were stored in potato cellars often built beneath the barn floor.   In one of the Drebley barns the floor has been lifted two or three feet and a doorway through this low wall leads into a vaulted cellar.   Nearby is a similar cellar excavated out of the hillside with an opening from the field above through which the potatoes were shot into the cellar.   The stonework and corbelled roofs retain a technique comparable to the Celtic beehive dwellings and the Welsh pigsties described so thoroughly by Peate.

5.   Constructional Details

(a)   The Timber Framework

THE cruck constructed buildings at Barden, Drebley and Bolton-by-Bowland consist of pairs of curved timbers set up in an inverted V form, the timbers meeting at the apex of the triangle so formed to produce a fork in which the ridge-tree rests. The rafters and purlins are placed on the crucks which therefore support the whole weight of the roof (Fig. 3). The walls of such buildings bear no relationship to the roof and serve only to enclose them.

The succeeding development was the king post truss set on teazle posts, a timber framework which characterises the larger barns such as those of Wigglesworth Hall and East Riddlesden Hall. Pairs of massive roughly-adzed oak trees, set butt uppermost on stone supports or stylobats, divide the building into bays exactly as did the pairs of crucks. A sturdy tie-beam rests on the top of each pair of teazle posts and from the centre of the tie-beam a vertical king-post carries the ridge pole. Curved struts spring out from the teazle-posts as extra support for the tie-beam (Fig. 10).

The carpentry of both cruck framework and teazle-post truss displays an honest simplicity. Each member is secured to the next by mortice and tenon joints firmly bound by oak pegs, so resulting in a structure beautiful in the fitness of its design. The framework was constructed on the ground and the local population turned out to help in "rearing the timbers," an event which was duly celebrated by feasting and drinking. The joints are often marked with Roman numerals or other symbols so that the timbers might be assembled correctly.

The later roof trusses rest on the walls which, therefore, carry the weight of the roof. An interesting transitional stage is provided by the roof truss at Cragg Farm, above Bingley, where the end of the tie-beam is supported by a short vertical upright resting on a stone sorbel projecting from the wall. Further support is afforded by a curved

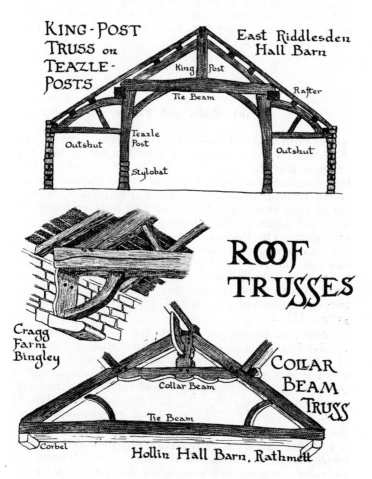

KING-POST TRUSS on TEAZLE-POSTS

East Riddlesden Hall Barn

King Post

Tie Beam

Rafter

Teazle Post

Outshut

Outshut

Stylobat

ROOF TRUSSES

Cragg Farm Bingley

COLLAR BEAM TRUSS

Collar Beam

Tie Beam

Corbel

Hollin Hall Barn, Rathmell

Fig. 10. Development of roof trusses.

bracket springing from the corbel (Fig. 10). Economy of timber resulted in a gradual impoverishment of the roof truss in the eighteenth century but they still often preserved a pleasing form. Such is the case with the collar beam truss at Hollin Hall Barn, Rathmell (Fig. 10). Collar beam and queen post trusses, in which two vertical uprights replaced the single king post, were in general use from the eighteenth century onwards.

(b) Walls and Floors

THE earliest Dales' buildings, the circular beehive huts of Grass Woods, were of rubble masonry, but it is probable that the majority of the first rectangular cruck-built houses had walls of wattle, woven in and out a number of vertical stakes and rendered waterproof by a coating of mud and straw or cow dung to produce the wattle and daub which persisted in some districts up to the present time. The balance sheets of Vicar Dytton provide our richest source of information on early Dales building and they contain several references to *watlying* in addition to the ones already quoted. "First, for repairs to the Tithe Barn at Otterburn for *watlying* bought and put on, for *thakke* bought and put on and *wallyng,* all reckoned together, 12s. 2d."

"Also paid for *watlyng* brought for the said houses (i.e., the dwelling house of Thom. Rakys in Ayrton and the barn of Thom. Paxton in Kyrkby) and for another building, viz. the barn of the said Raks:— First to the Abbot of Sallay for 4 loads bought, 20d., and for carrying and felling two loads of the same 2s. 4d. Also for 4 loads bought from Milrakys Clyf, 28d., and for filling and *beryng owt* 2s. Also for carrying the same, 3s."

Unfortunately we have no proof that the "watlyng" was employed for the walls and the mention of "wallyng" as a separate item appears to indicate that the two were not synonymous. Peate quotes a number of references to the use of wattle as a foundation for a thatch of heather or rushes in Wales:—

"At Tal-y-llyn the roofs are wattled."

"The roof was made by placing timbers from the wall-plate up to the ridge piece on both sides; they were woven

Hollow Chamfer   Splay   Ogee
17th. Century Mullions

Staircase
Window
Nappa Hall

WINDOWS

Hall
Window
Nappa Hall

Barn
"Laap
-Hoils"

Barden Scale   East Riddlesden

Fig. 11. Typical features of early windows.

to the ridge piece with withes. Strong withes were placed across them and the roof was then generally thatched with rushes."

Was this the purpose of the "watlyng" bought for the house of Thomas Rakys? Against this supposition is the fact that "watlyng" and "thakking" two houses cost 18s. 4d., whereas walling a house cost 4s. 6d. Had the entire walls been of stone one would have expected the cost to have been considerably higher, and in addition the quantity of "watlyng" bought seems excessive for underthatching alone. Most probably the lower part of the walls was of stone and the upper part of wattle and daub after the manner of the so-called "half-timbered" houses which still survive in many districts.

Walls of turf blocks or of rubble masonry with the interstices filled with turf replaced the wattle and daub, but in the sixteenth century dressed stone set in mortar became more widespread. Even so, dressed sandstone was reserved for the cornerstones, jambs, mullions, lintels, and similar features whilst the walls themselves were of river boulders or undressed stones built with a rubble filling. Lime, obtained from the village kiln, and sand comprised the mortar. Inside, the walls were often plastered and whitened but the bedrooms, until quite recent times, were coloured blue with orchil or brown with yellow ochre and often had a simple border consisting of spots and a wavy line.

The earlier floors were of beaten earth, but flagstones, thick slabs of fissile sandstone similar to thakstones, are now almost universal. The proud Yorkshire housewife has always insisted on spotlessly clean floors and the flagstones both inside and out were invariably scrubbed weekly, scoured with sand and rubbed over with yellow rubble or even washed with milk to yield a dark, glossy surface. The hearthstone, with its surrounding wooden fender, was the object of greatest attention, and even during the earlier years of the present century it was always decorated with a maze of pattern in white "pot mould" (Fig. 15). Similar decoration was often applied to the doorstep and to the "flags" leading up to the door and in the more remote parts of northern Scotland the practice was extended even to the cow byres. In later years the patterns were purely decorative but they are a survival of a much older superstitious custom. The threshold and hearth are the two parts of a house almost universally considered by primitive people as regions especially subject to

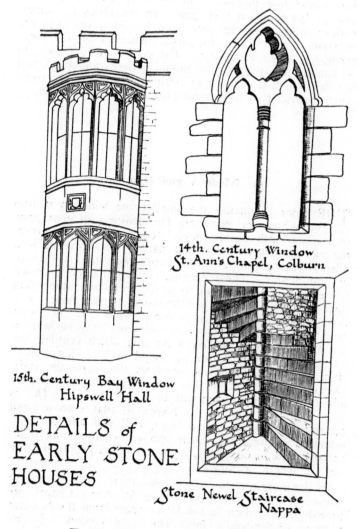

14th. Century Window
St. Ann's Chapel, Colburn

15th. Century Bay Window
Hipswell Hall

DETAILS of
EARLY STONE
HOUSES

Stone Newel Staircase
Nappa

Fig. 12. Details of early stone houses.

the activities of evil spirits. By surrounding these with a maze of pattern they hoped that any such malignant visitors would lose themselves in the intricacies of the lines and so fail to reach their goal. In the Dales the superstitious origin has long since been forgotten and even the patterns are now but treasured memories of the older members of our generation. The clean sanded floor with its rubbled hearthstone, pot mould patterns and blackened wooden fender lent an air of fresh homeliness to the room which provided its own reward for the labour entailed.

(c) Windows and Doorways

THE older the house the smaller the windows is true throughout the Pennines. The dearness of glass prior to the sixteenth century prohibited its use by all except the richest householders, and narrow slits covered with oiled linen, horn or reed wickerwork, were the only source of illumination. These openings served mainly to permit the escape of smoke and to admit fresh air rather than light, a theory which is substantiated by the name "window" itself meaning — as it does, "wind eye," or "wind hole." Survivals of such early windows may be seen in the narrow vertical or triangular slits which ventilate the older barns and are known as "laap-hoils" or "lowp-holes" (Fig. 11). Similar narrow windows illuminate the staircase of Nappa Hall but they are deeply splayed within to admit the maximum amount of light (Fig. 11). This is true of all the windows at Nappa so that even a small opening passing through a thick wall still afforded considerable illumination. Such splayed windows almost invariably had window seats, a custom which prevailed up to the eighteenth century.

Of the more pretentious windows, those of the old manor house at Colburn, now known as St. Ann's Chapel, are probably the earliest in the Dales apart from the Norman windows of Scolland's Hall. The south window is divided by a round shaft into two lights resulting in a window almost identical with the thirteenth-century windows of Little Wenham Hall, Suffolk, the mid fourteenth-century windows of the Fish House, Meare, Somerset, and the late fourteenth-century windows of the Manor House, Mar-

Porch with Pigeon Loft
Malham   1617

17th. Cent. Pegged Door
East Riddlesden Hall Barn.

DOORS
and
DOORWAYS

Farnhill

HAL 1692

Deepdale

Newby

RLC ↓
1632 HB   Arncliffe

16th. and 17th. Century
Doorheads

Water Gate Barn, Barden.

Fig. 13. Some Dales doorways and doorheads.

tock, in the same county (Fig. 12). Markenfield Hall has fourteenth-century windows which show a more advanced stage of development similar to the cusped windows of Nappa. Nappa Hall has two-light or three-light windows, cusped and with mullions of the hollow chamfer type (Fig. 11). Even in these instances glass was rare and wooden shutters with iron grilles protected the openings.

Hipswell Hall's two-storeyed bay has five equal sides, with a double-cusped ogee arch and square-headed light on each, to form a window of considerable beauty (Fig. 12). The fifteenth-century gatehouse, known as Marmion's Tower, which is all that remains of the Manor Place at Tanfield, also has a delightful oriel window with two lights on each of the three sides, each light having a double cusped head with tracery above.

With the advent of cheaper glass towards the end of the sixteenth century the long mullioned windows became one of the dominant features of the Dales' house. The hollow chamfer mullion persisted until the early part of the seventeenth century when it was succeeded by the normal flat chamfer or splay type which, in its turn, gave way to the curved ogee section by the middle of the century (Fig. 11).

The doorways of this region are of particular interest, especially in the variety and nature of the door head which is characterised by a deep stone lintel on which the owner's initials, the date of building and occasionally a sundial or some crude ornamentation are engraved. This feature is more pronounced in Craven, Wharfedale and Ribblesdale, particularly around Settle, where the beauty of the design is often spoilt by over-elaboration. In the early sixteenth century examples, such as that from an outbuilding at Farnhill which now forms part of a sunken garden wall at Farnhill Hall, the date and the initials of the owner and his wife are each placed in separate rectangles sunk in a plain headstone (Fig. 13). In later examples the initials are combined, that of the surname being carved first, followed by those of the christian names of the owner and his wife (Fig. 13). Rarely the initials of the builder are included as in the Arncliffe example (Fig. 13)., described by Raistrick, where R indicates the surname and L and C the christian names of the owners, whereas H.B. was the builder. The simple mouldings of the jambs are carried up on to the lintel where they form square, arched or round-headed panels. A porch, with stone benches on each side, often protects the doorway and this may be two-

17th. Century Door
Bolton Peel

Fig. 14. Early boarded door, Bolton Peel, Bolton by-Bowland.

storeyed with a small chamber and sometimes a pigeon loft above the entrance as in William Preston's house in Malham (Fig. 13). Pigeons were an important item of food in the days when only salted meat could be obtained during the winter months, and pigeon lofts occupy many a gable end in both house and barn. A tiny room above the porch of Bolton Peel served as a "powdering closet."

The door itself was a solid boarded structure even in William Dytton's time for his balance sheet includes an item of 22d. "for making the doors of the said house, and the houses of Thom. Paxton and Ric. Arnald." An excellent seventeenth-century boarded door, the boards of which are secured by oak pegs, is still preserved in the old barn at East Riddlesden Hall (Fig. 13). The main house door of Bolton Peel is of the same period and it also consists of a number of stout oak boards pegged together. It swings on a pair of delightfully wrought iron hinges fashioned, no doubt, by the local blacksmith, and it is secured by a massive lock (Fig. 14). A wooden wedge hanging from a piece of cord is used as a further protection, being wedged above the latch. The yeoman farmer of Bolton Peel must have valued his treasures very highly for even these protections weren't considered sufficient. Two recesses, one in each jamb, accommodated a stout oak bar which was slid into position at night. Fomerly most doors were fastened by means of such a wooden stang and Darnbrook House and Coleby Hall, near Askrigg, are among the many houses where the occupants were rendered safe from intruders by this means.

In the early stone houses circular stone newel staircases were general, leading from the ground floor up to the roof of the tower, as at Nappa and Markenfield (Fig. 12). The Markenfield example is surmounted by a mediaeval conical cap. A wooden Jacob's ladder afforded access to the upper loft of the more humble dwelling. In the seventeenth-century yeoman farmer's house the staircase leading from the hall was often an ornate oak structure with turned and carved balusters and newels. Occasionally the bottom of the stairs was provided with a pair of dog-gates to prevent the household dogs from straying upstairs.

(d) Roofs

ALTHOUGH we have no supporting documentary evidence it seems likely that the earliest Dales' buildings were thatched. Vicar Dytton's balance sheet has a number of references to the purchase of "thakke" and "thakkyng" and, as stone slates were referred to in early accounts as "thakstones," we may assume that "thakke" is a term applied to thatching material such as straw or ling. The old barns and houses of Barden, Drebley, Hurst and Colsterdale are still thatched with turf and ling, but the craft of heather thatching is almost dead and the majority of these buildings are now untenanted and fast falling into ruin. Others have been saved by a roofing of corrugated iron laid on a bedding of ling.

The ling roof rests on closely spaced rafters consisting of roughly split branches stretching from the top of the side walls to the ridge-tree against which they are secured by wooden pegs. They are steeply pitched, usually about 60°, and the ridges are often capped with slabs of turf pegged to the underlying thatch. According to Addy, turf used for this purpose was known as "dovet" in the north of England, but so far I have been unable to find anyone in the Dales who is familiar with the term. Crump has collected the name "flaughts" from the Halifax district, and he quotes a letter from a Mrs. Broadbent of Sowerby, stating that she remembers her mother saying that they sometimes used to "theyk wi' flaughts" (thatch with flaughts). Addy also points out that some contrivance would be necessary to prevent the turf from falling down, especially before it had grown together, and amongst the Norsemen this was known as a *torf-völr,* a thick plank which ran along the eaves. In the Dales' buildings the side walls are capped by a double course of stone slates projecting a few inches over the wall top and these form a base on which the ling and turf rest.

Only a few thatched buildings now remain in the Dales. The fear of fire resulted in most cottages being re-roofed with stone slates, and with this change commenced the decline in the thatcher's craft. Details of the methods are fortunately still remembered, for thatching in the Dales differed from that in other parts of the country. A foundation of wheat straw, tied into bundles, or "battens," was laid on the rafters one batten deep. Young straight ling was then placed on top of the straw, starting at the eaves and working upwards. This was pulled and the adhering soil allowed to remain. The soil acted as "backin'" — "You need plenty o' 'backin'," one old Colsterdale thatcher told me. After a few courses had been laid the thatch was weighted with stones and allowed to settle down before being pegged to the under-thatch. Subsequent layers were added in similar stages until the whole roof was covered, when long strips of turf were placed across the ridge and pegged down. In the more humble barns the straw foundation is apparently always omitted and the ling rests directly on the rafters.

The more pretentious dwellings were roofed with stone slates, or "thakstones," as early as the twelfth century, but no widespread application of this roofing material was noticeable until the sixteenth and seventeenth centuries when stone replaced timber and thatch in all but the humbler dwellings. Many of the Wharfedale farmsteads have only been re-roofed in the last century and in odd corners the ling roof still survives. These roofing slates are fissile flagstones quarried either from the Middle and Lower Coal Measures; from beds near the base of the Millstone Grit, or from flags below and above the Simonstone Limestone. The Coal Measure roofing slates are only used in Airedale. According to Raistrick, most of the Dales' thackstones are quarried near Hawes, Askrigg, and Carperby in Wensleydale, near Low Reeth in Swaledale, and near Beckermonds in Langstrothdale. A few localities in Coverdale supplied much of mid-Wharfedale with flags, also from above and below the Simonstone Limestone. Millstone Grit flags were quarried on Mallerstang Edge near Keld, and on Fountains Fell. The "Hawes Flags" are finer grained, smoother and thinner and are used in larger sizes.

The blocks of fissile sandstone are split by a slate striker, a craft now almost obsolete, and graded into various sizes which are measured with a "wippett stick." The various sizes were formerly given picturesque names, the following being typical of the Pennine region:—

10½ inches.	Scant Fairwells.
12	,,	Fairwells.
13½	,,	Scant Short Skirtchens.
15	,,	Short Skirtchens.
16½	,,	Scant Long Skirtchens.
18	,,	Long Skirtchens.
19½	,,	Scant Short Becks.
21	,,	Short Becks.

22½	,,	Scant Long Becks.
24	,,	Long Becks.
25½	,,	Scant Batchelors.
27	,,	Batchelors.
28½	,,	Scant Wivetts, Wibbetts or Wippetts.
30	,,	Wivetts.
31½	,,	Scant Twelves.
33	,,	Twelves.
34½	,,	Scant Thirteens.
36	,,	Thirteens.

Stone slate roofs are widespread not only throughout the Pennines but also in the Cotswolds, in Sussex and in the Lake District. The Cotswold and Pennine types have much in common although they also display marked differences due to the nature of the slates employed and to the prevailing styles of local architecture. The essential differences lie in the flatter pitches of the Pennine houses.

The slates are hung on a roof framework of stout oak rafters pegged together and battened with split oak or small branches arranged to accommodate the diminishing slate courses. In hanging the slates, oak pegs are commonly driven through one hole, although two may be seen, at the head of the slate. Occasionally they are nailed, tied or even pegged with sheep shank bones or antler tines.

The "cussome," "counter" or under-eave slate is bedded in mortar directly on the wall at a pitch up to 15°. The largest slates are employed for the first course and, in order to enable the tails of the slates to fit closely against the slates below, stone wedges or packing are inserted between the counters and the "house" course. These supplement the action of the counters which cause the slates to bend on their tails and they afford additional support to the centres of the large slates which would otherwise tend to break during repairs.

This employment of the cussome or counter ensures better protection against the wind and rain, affording a tighter joint, and it also gives a peculiar concave outline to the verge of a gable. Such a "bellcast" appearance is due partly to a tendency of the heavy roofs to sag inwards and also to the gradual increase in pitch towards the ridge, produced by the employment of the cussome. It will be obvious, too, that the pitch of the rafter will be steeper than the gable slope. In the Cotswolds the pitch varies between 45° and 55° but in the Pennines the average pitch is between 35° and 40° although the earlier ling thatched roofs were as steep as 60°. This difference in pitch of the stone slate roofs is primarily due to the different kinds of slates employed. The Cotswold slates are both smaller and lighter, giving less lap and demanding a steeper pitch to ensure a watertight roof. It is almost certain that the angles finally adopted were the result of considerable experiment before the most efficient slope could be determined.

The slates of the eaves or "house" course, often measure two feet or more in width and have a corresponding length, and the succeeding courses diminish gradually to a width of about eight inches. The laps also diminish from about three inches to an inch and at the ridge the slates are finished with a hewn stone "cresting" or ridge piece in the form of a plain saddleback. In the more remote regions of the north-west, "wrestler slates," cut with a notch so that they interlock right along the ridge, are sometimes employed to complete the ridge.

The eaves rarely project more than six inches beyond the wall face, whilst the projection of the verges is about half that amount. The verges of the gables are quite often finished with a coping, or "tabling," which is applied in one of two ways. In one method the coping is bedded directly on to the slates which pass right through to the front wall. The edges of the slates and the wall immediately below are pointed. In the alternative method the coping is bedded directly to the stonework, the coping stones being unbonded except at the ridge and eaves. In this case the slates are tucked into rebate at the back of the coping. The Yorkshire coping stones are often mitred, the plain and hollow chamfer being usually employed, and at the eaves the coping is cranked to allow the water to be thrown clear of the wall. After the seventeenth century these cranked copings were gradually made narrower, thereby losing all their original quality.

Valleys are invariably produced by means of mitred slates overlapping a series of slates arranged as a gutter. Lead was used only rarely by Dales' builders prior to the eighteenth century except in some of the larger halls such as the east wing of Nappa Hall and Skipton Castle. Both of these have lead gutters and rainwater spouts; those at Skipton bearing the arms of Clifford and Veteripont in addition to the letters A.P. (Anne Pembroke) and the date

1659. The absence of lead for flashings was a source of great trouble to the early builder, especially at the joints of sloping roof surfaces and vertical walls or at the junctions of roofs and chimney-stacks. Occasionally the joint is merely pointed but in some cases it is protected still further by a series of almost vertical slates known as "weather-stones." In other instances a series of step-like thakstones projects from the wall to cover the joint. These are known as "crow steps." In order to reduce such joints to a minimum the Dales' slater adopted the practice of employing unequal pitches, and it is quite common to find a long sweeping roof reaching almost to the ground in order to cover the mistal or kitchen.

One of the most remarkable features of these early roofs is the wide variety of the finials which surmount the gables and terminate the kneelers as at Burnsall Grammar School and East Riddlesden Hall. Of particular interest is the example on a group of cottages at Beckfoot, Cottingley, which is in the form of a stone lantern. This was the badge used by the Knights Templars and their successors, the Knights of St. John of Jerusalem, to distinguish their own property, for all property belonging to these two Orders was exempt from tithes.

The early roofs had very little pointing apart from the cresting and one or two courses immediately below the verges and the eaves. This had to be frequently renewed and it was, and still is, invariably whitened to provide a most pleasing appearance. Later the joints were also pointed from the inside but this was not widespread until last century and labourers who slept in the attics often work in the morning to find themselves covered with snow which had blown in through the slates. To render the roof more weatherproof sphagnum moss was stuffed in between the slates by means of a mossing iron and the late continuance of this practice is indicated by the church-wardens' accounts for the parish of Stalling Busk, near Semerwater, from which the following extracts are taken:—

1802-3	To lime and liming and mossing the Chapel	7s.	0d.
	Mossing and getting moss . .	2s.	6d.
1805-6	Liming, plasteing, mossing and whitewashing the Chapel . .	10s.	0d.

The mellow rich red tiles which roof many a house in the villages lower down the Dales are of a relatively recent date for, although tiles were favoured by the Romans, stone slates and thatch are undoubtedly the traditional roofing materials of the Pennine slopes. An interesting feature, not confined to the Dales, is the employment of two or three courses of stone slates immediately above the eaves, whilst the remainder of the roof is tiled. This is done apparently so that a ladder may be rested against the eaves without any fear of breaking the more fragile tiles.

(e) Hearth and Chimney

IN the prehistoric beehive dwelling an open hearth stood near the centre of the floor, and in the house body of Blackburn Hall at Grinton the large seventeenth century fireplace is situated some distance from the end wall, the space behind having been converted into a small store-room almost identical with the arrangement in the Saxon house. The fact that the fireplace and chimney are both dated, whereas there is no date on the stone lintel, seems to indicate that both were built in the year 1635 to replace an open hearth situated in the middle of the floor, and Addy has suggested that this was the normal position in the Middle Ages. In the most humble cottages the smoke made its exit through an opening in the roof but in the more substantial dwellings canopies or louvres of wattle smeared with a mixture of clay and cow dung served to conduct the smoke. Dr. Raistrick mentions a chimney of wattle daubed with clay which existed in Threshfield until quite recently. Even in the early sixteenth century the chimney carried up the side of the wall was a rarity, for Leland, writing in 1538, says of Bolton Castle, "One thinge I muche notyd in the haulle of Bolton, how chimneys were conveyed by tunnells made on the syds of the wauls, betwixt the lights in the haull; and by this means, and by no covers, is the smoke of the harthe wonder strangly conveyed." Early external stone chimneys are a common feature of the Dales' buildings as in the cottage at Club Nook and the Old Hall at Barden, near Bellerby. Chimney-pots are a still more recent feature, the common practice being to cover the chimney-top either by means of two stone slates sloping to meet each other at the apex or a single flagstone raised on a small stone at each corner.

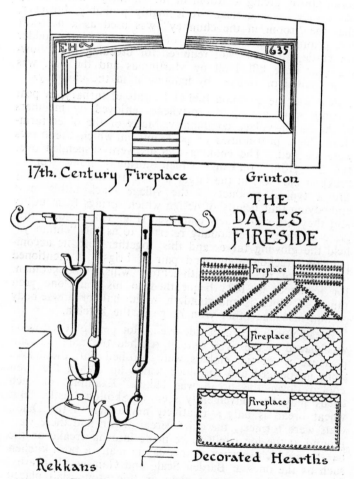

17th. Century Fireplace   Grinton

THE
DALES
FIRESIDE

Rekkans   Decorated Hearths

Fig. 15. The Dales fireside and its fittings.

The sixteenth century saw the introduction of large open hearths with extensive chimney-breasts often carved and bearing the date, as at Blackburn Hall (Fig. 15). In some houses the chimney-breasts projected several feet into the room above, giving a "room in the chimney" which Addy has decided was useless. It is highly probably, however, that the "room in the chimney" was used as a beef-loft for, prior to the introduction of turnips as winter fodder for cattle, all stocks not required for breeding the following year were killed off by Martinmas and the beef was either salted or smoked by hanging it in the chimney.

Peat was the common fuel and rights of turbary, or peat cutting, were among the privileges enjoyed by members of the Saxon village community. Many of the older farmsteads have peat-houses or peat-coits in which the turves were stacked. The cooking utensils were suspended over the fire from "rekkans" which normally hung from a "rekkan bar" or, in the larger houses, from a crane. They are a typical product of the village blacksmith's craft embodying that beauty of design which springs from utility and they are still widely employed (Fig. 15). A loose fire-grate or range, occasionally referred to as the "chimney," held the glowing turves and this, together with its accompanying "reckon, tongs and pair of brigs," is mentioned in many of the seventeenth-century wills. One yeoman, for instance, in 1623 bequeathed to his son "one yron range — which is and standeth in the hall or howse-body — and also one other yron range in the kytchin."

Bread was baked in a side-oven. Hot peat or oven-wood was placed in the oven until it reached the required tempearture when the embers were brushed out, the loaves were introduced and the door sealed up. When the oven cooled down the bread was baked. Examples of such ovens may be conveniently seen in Skipton Castle. But wheat bread is only a relatively newcomer to the Dales. Oats were formerly the chief cereal grown and these were ground at the local mill to be made into havercake on the bakstone which survives to this day in many a farm kitchen such as the ones at Barden Scale and Gamsworth nearby. This was either a metal plate or thin stone slab placed over a separate fireplace. The oatmeal was mixed with water in a wooden trough, or "knade-kit," and the mixture was then poured on to a wooden board covered with muslin, the "bak-brade," from which it was transferred to the bakstone. After a few seconds the havercake was turned by means of a wooden "spittle." Then, whilst still in a moist state, it was hung over the "bread-creel" or "bread-fleak" to dry. Havercake was the staple food throughout the whole Pennine region until a century or so ago.

BIBLIOGRAPHY

Addy, S. O.:
  The Evolution of the English House. 1910.

Ambler, Louis:
  Old Halls and Manor Houses of Yorkshire. 1913.

Crump, W. B.:
  "The Little Hill Farm," in *Proc. Halifax Antiquarian Society,* 1938 pp. 115-196.

Crump, W. B.:
  "The Yeoman Clothier of the Seventeenth Century: His Home and His Loom Shop," in *The Bradford Antiquary,* Pt. 25, New Series, Vol. V. 1932, pp. 217-239.

Ford, T. F.:
  "Some Buildings of the Seventeenth Century in the Parish of Halifax," in Thoresby Society's *Miscellanea,* Vol. XXVIII, 1928, pp. 1-64.

Goodall, A.:
  Place Names of South-West Yorkshire, 1914.

Innocent, C. F.:
  The Development of English Building Construction, 1916.

Lloyd, Nathaniel:
  A history of the English House. 1931.

Morkill, J. W.:
  The Parish of Kirkby Malhamdale. 1933.

Peate, Iorwerth C.:
  "The Welsh House," in *Y Cymmrodor,* Vol. XLVII., 1940.

Raistrick, Arthur:
  "Dales Building of the Sixteenth and Seventeenth Centuries," in *The Yorkshire Dalesman,* Vol. III, 1941.

Raistrick, A. and Chapman, S. E. :
"The Lynchet Groups of Upper Wharfedale, York-shire," in *Antiquity,* June 1929, pp. 165-181.

Sanderson, Gordon :
Architectural Features of the Settle District.

Thompson, A. Hamilton :
The English House. 1936.

Walton, James :
"The Timberwork of English Barn Buildings," in *Country Life,* 19 June, 1942, pp. 1180-1.

Walton, James :
"South Pennine Barn Buildings," in *The Architectural Review,* Vol. XC., 1941, pp. 122-4.

Walton, James :
"The Tithe Barns of Yorkshire," in *Notes and Queries,* Vol. 181, 1941, pp. 340-1.

Walton, James :
"The Stone Slate Roofs of England," in *The Quarry Managers' Journal,* 1941, pp. 64-66 and 93-96.

Walton, James :
"Hogback Tombstones and the Homes of the Vik-ings," in *The Quarry Managers' Journal,* 1946, pp. 201-5.

Wood, Margaret :
"Norman Domestic Architecture," in *The Archaeolo-gical Journal,* Vol. XCII, 1936, pp. 167-242.

Readers wishing to refer to an up-to-date bibliography of publications should consult **A Bibliography on Vern-acular Architecture,** edited by Sir Robert De Zouche Hall and published by David & Charles, Newton Abbot, 1972.